STEAMPUNK JEWELRY

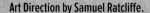

Art Direction by Samuel Ratcliffe.

Published in 2014 by Graffito Books Ltd, 32 Great Sutton Street, London EC1V 0NB, UK
www.graffbooks.co.uk
© Graffito Books Ltd, 2014.
ISBN 978-1909051041

British Library cataloguing-in-publication data:
A catalogue record of this book is available at the British Library.

Printed in China.

STEAMPUNK JEWELRY

Spurgeon Vaughn Ratcliffe

GRAFFITO

CONTENTS

APPENDIX

FOREWORD

After my foray into the world of steampunk fashion, I slept for 200 days, until on
the evening of the 201st day, I was wakened by an unusual piercing blue light through my
bedroom window. Looking out over Tempelhof Field I saw the old airstrip flooded with light,
illuminated by the biggest and bluest moon I had ever set eyes on in some 300 years of time
travel. On turning on my aethergraph communication device, I saw that an object had been
transmuted to me, along with a note, from none other than Blue Moon Designs. This was
clearly a sign marking the beginning of a new adventure. I held the object in my hands; it was
a brooch which gave off a sumptuously eery glow. The attached message read: 'Take this to the
subterranean garden beneath Tempelhof Field. Use the light to guide you. Your transport, a
Bionic Unicorn awaits." And so it began. I grabbed my brass flying goggles, donned my leather
flying jacket, hoisted my steampack on my back, and I was off.

I entered the subterranean garden through an old hatch in the airstrip. It was pitch black, but
slowly my brooch turned on and I could just discern a well-worn path. In the far distance,
through vines and brambles, was a faint, multicolored glow. As I headed through the thicket,
I noticed the bushes were dripping with glass jewels and adorned with beautiful butterflies
crafted from a variety of metals of the most delectable colors. I headed towards the glow once
more and, as I got closer, I noticed that the glowing object was remarkably small, a German
'Rauten Jewel' indeed, famed for its magical glistening properties. Just then, from behind the
bushes, emerged the aforementioned bionic unicorn. As it approached it transmogrified into
a female human form; I quickly recognized Kristin Berwald, of Bionic Unicorn, famed crafter
of the finest steampunk jewelry. It was then that I realized my new mission would involve
the exploration of the finer details of the Victorian futurist aesthetic, from all corners of our
glistening round earth: the art of steampunk jewelry.

Kristin concurred and took trouble to explain to me the essential aspects of her art and craft,
and told of other metal smiths and purveyors of steampunk treasures. I was to start my
explorations at the very heart of the movement, setting off to find the studio of the renowned
Steel Hip Designs, whose mastercrafter, Michelle Murray, would show me devices I could
only dream of. Our conversation complete, Kristin took her leave, disappearing back into
the thicket. Almost simultaneously the splitting image of the first unicorn sprang from the
undergrowth behind. It too was bionic; outwardly flesh, I could yet hear the whirring of gears
and the gentle hiss of escaping steam through its nostrils as it moved. I swiftly mounted and
off it galloped at an astounding speed. As we emerged onto Templehof airstrip the beast sprung
giant metallic wings and we soared, heading straight towards the now gigantic blue moon.

We set down in Perth, Australasia with thuds, galloping and huge clouds of dust as we grinded to a halt. The giant beast practically threw me to the ground before shooting off once more into the dawn sun. Between the palm trees, skyscrapers and micro-bikini clad and budgie-smuggling bathers, stood Steel Hip Designs' studio. I was greeted by the charming Michelle, a genius in copper construction, and the creator of the piece which would grace the cover of the book of my adventures – her *Mechanical Heart* pendant. After a disquisition on her methods and, inspired by Murray's industriousness and tenacity, I built a mono passenger steam micro-airship to take me on the rest of my journey.

I arrived first in the Golden State. Here I discovered the wonderland that is Elaina Louise Studios, with hot air balloon-inspired creations, Lucky Steampunk with her brilliant use of vintage timepieces, the elegant clockworks of Amber Ilys Steamcrafts, Steamy Tech's remarkable laser beam-cut wooden gears and the 'sightmares' of Dr. Brassy Steamington. After a short detour to the royal kingdom of Hawaii, and a visit to my very talented old friend Friston, I returned to the Americas, to the enlightened state of Oregon where I was truly inspired by Steampunk Nation and Swank Metalsmithing. Then East to the fast-growing city of Detroit, to see the stunning Raven Eve, before I swooped to Montgomeryville, PA to investigate the wonderful, frequently winged creations of Mechanique Steampunk. Even though my French was a little rusty, it was time to head north again to Quebec and the royal city of Montreal, where reside both the worker of very fine gold, palladium and silver, Claudio Pino, and the very influential Daniel Proulx, of Catherinette Rings.

Having had enough of flying, I returned to the old continent by fast steam packet, sailing first through the Mediterranean to the emerging city of Tel Aviv to be astonished and excited by the dark, sexy creations of Orions Factory. Then north I went, by ship first to Trieste, one of my favorite cities, and thence by high-speed iron horse, to see Jazz Steampunk in the Netherlands. After taking the air and the waters at Scheveningen, I crossed to the country that first tamed the power of steam, Great Britain, and to the wonderful forge of Fran Horne in the ancient cathedral city of Worcester. Her shop, Curiouser and Curiouser, perfectly defined my sense of all that I had seen on my travels, and her works of amber and resin cast a warm glow as I later sat by her fire, sipping an ancient Malmsey wine, secure in the knowledge that my journey had proved, to me at least, that no more creative force in the creation of jewelry exists than the heavenly aesthetic of steampunk.

"I love the multiplicity of Steampunk" says Amber Ily, "there are so many different styles within it. You can go Victorian and add a bit of steam, or you can go post-apocalyptic." Amber Ily grew up reading H.G. Wells and Jules Verne, and got into steampunk fashion about ten years ago. Today she works with watch parts, door knockers and skeleton keys. For her tools, it's steel jewelry pliers, E-6000 glue and a welder. Her workspace is decorated with a steampunk gun, a taxidermy bat, spider, baby shark, goggles and an ancient typewriter. "Inspiration comes from found objects and anything Alice in Wonderland – I love to mix the latter and steampunk." Based in Temecula, CA, Amber Ily has to travel to steampunk events, notably the gaslight gathering in San Diego every year. "The scene has grown dramatically since I started. It's hard to imagine how many books, movies, jewelry designers, fashion designers there are out there. It's wonderful. The creativity of the movement and fans will ensure it keeps growing. We're not going anywhere soon."

FAR LEFT: *Alice in Wonderland Doorknocker*, necklace. Vintage door knocker, copper chain, vintage teapot charm.
ABOVE: *Doorknocker Watch Face*, necklace. Vintage door knocker, copper chain, vintage watch face.
LEFT: Amber Ily wearing *Octopus Necklace*.

ABOVE: *Alice in Wonderland March Hare*, necklace. Copper chain, vintage broken watch, March hare pendant.
LEFT: *Steampunk Octopus*, necklace. Vintage watch parts, octopus pendant, copper chain, bolts.

LEFT: *Doorknocker with Watch Movement*, necklace.
Vintage door knocker, vintage watch movement,
copper chain.
ABOVE: *Black Doorknocker with Watch Movement*,
necklace. Black door knocker, silver chain, vintage
watch movement.

Working out of a "subterranean forest lair" Bionic Unicorn, aka Kristin Berwald, aims to create jewelry that makes people "feel like magical steampunk badass stars as they go about their adventures." Her workshop, she says, is very much like her mind: "I'm one of those 'Method to Madness' sorts. If you stepped into my studio you would see enamel flowers arranged by colour, sorted watch parts and mechanical oddities, but then an explosion of rainbows and in-progress works. Kind of like a Salvador Dalì painting." She has a particular love of cuckoo clocks, and wanted to make jewelry that suggested the insides and outsides of the clocks mixed up. "Symbols of creation and deconstruction are very appealing to me. My creativity works like a web, where I trap data about art history, world culture and science fiction; then I weave it all together while processing it through my steampunk fairytale filter." Kristin's work has been extensively featured in shows at the Minneapolis Institute of Arts, First Ave, TeslaCon and the Walker Art Center. It has also appeared in magazines such as *Dark Beauty*, *Gothic Beauty* and *Mpls/St Paul*. Justin Bieber is just one of her many clients. Of her local steampunk scene she says: "It's awesome. I collaborate with designers like Blasphemina's Closet and KMK Designs, and some amazing photographers and models, who share a common vision of the movement."

LEFT: *Aurora Borealis Crest*, necklace. Symmetrical brass scrolls, antique watch movements, Swarovski crystals, West German 'Rauten Rose' jewel, vintage glass jewels.
ABOVE: Steampunk butterfly necklaces. Watch gears, antique watch movements, flowers, and Swarovski crystals.

LEFT: *Nachtvlinder*, necklace. Gold and rose gold enamel, Swarovski crystals, vintage watch parts.
ABOVE: *The Oracle*, necklace. Silver plate, Swarovski crystals, gold and copper antiquing, antique watch movement, vintage gears.

ABOVE: *The Oracle*, necklace (detail). Materials as before.
RIGHT: *Dark Triumph*, necklace. Silver, antique watch movements, West German crystals, Swarovski crystals, rhinestones.

ABOVE and RIGHT: *Copper Bramble*, necklace. Black and rose gold enamel, vintage brass, antique watch plate (Waltham, 1889), Swarovski crystals, Avon Rambling Rose chain.

ABOVE: *Nachtvindler*, necklace (detail); materials as before.
RIGHT: *Clockwork Queen of Chaos*, necklace. Red enamel, gears, acrylic, brass, Swarovski crystals, antiqued brass chain.

LEFT: *Watchful Eye*, brooch. Recycled vacuum tube, LED light, resin cameos, antique watch parts, metal charms.
ABOVE: *Green Monster Eye*, brooch. Recycled vacuum tube, LED light, resin cameos, antique watch parts, metal charms.

"The thing that inspires most about steampunk is the clever hacks and mods, for instance Datamancer's or Jake Von Slatt's work. I also love my friend Kimric Smythe's boilers, which he constructs from victorian-era manuals," says Oakland-based Katherine Becvar of Blue Moon Designs. She first discovered the movement at the Burning Man Festival in 2007: "It blew my mind, I just had to get involved." She talked her way into the Neverwas Haul crew and now works with them at Burning Man and in the Bay Area on events like the Mad Hatter Art Car Parade and the Obtainium Cup Contraptor's Rally. That work, she says, is her main source of inspiration. Katherine creates her jewelry from the former garage of her house. Her signature style uses old vacuum tubes, which she lights up with LEDs. "To me the juxtaposition of the antique/old/obsolete and cutting edge/new captures the essence of steampunk."

BELOW: *Laboratory Assortment*, brooch. Recycled vacuum tube, LED light, resin cameos, antique watch parts, metal charms.

RIGHT: *Keeping Time*, brooch. Recycled vacuum tube, LED light, resin cameos, antique watch parts, metal charms.

BELOW: *The Neverwas Haul Rides Again*, brooch. Recycled vacuum tube, LED light, resin cameos, antique watch parts, metal charms.
LEFT: *From the Deeps*, brooch. Recycled vacuum tube, LED light, resin cameos, antique watch parts, metal charms.

LEFT: *Winged Flower*, brooch. Recycled vacuum tube, LED light, resin cameos, antique watch parts, metal charms.

BELOW: *My Heart Fills with Adoration*, brooch. Recycled vacuum tube, LED light, resin cameos, antique watch parts, metal charms.

Montreal-based Daniel Proulx remembers starting out in 2008. "At the time there was no steampunk community in my city, but I knew that there were people who were interested in the movement. Eventually we made contact and Steampunk Montreal, which encourages creativity in the genre in all its forms, was the result." It started as just a bit of fun, copying his partner Catherine as she made wire rings. His own take was to make retro-futuristic designs, which a friend suggested were rather 'steampunk' – "that was the first time I had heard the term." When he started showing more work, the response from around the world was so positive that he quit his job to concentrate on steampunk full-time. A few months later he was invited to be part of the first steampunk exhibition at the Museum of Science in Oxford: "It was amazing to be shown there, amongst so many talented artists." The Victorian era is the great inspiration, in particular that unique melding of science and art. "Inventors then took the time to make things beautiful; the sheer craftsmanship is what is so inspiring." Six years on, Daniel has now sold his work in 39 countries (including Monaco, Latvia, Israel, Indonesia, Singapore and Japan), has been featured in exhibitions at Kew, London and at the Mark Twain museum in the US, and has seen his work being used on book covers (for Neil Gaiman) and on TV (*The Warehouse Show*).

LEFT: *Steampunk Mad Scientist Ring.* Copper, watch movement, reptile taxidermy glass eye, amber, findings.
ABOVE: *Steampunk Ring with Clock Parts Inlayed in Amber.* Clock parts, amber, copper, findings.

LEFT: *Steampunk Tie Tack.* Taxidermy glass eye,
clock parts, findings.
ABOVE: *Steampunk Airship Pirate Ring.* Taxidermy
glass eye, copper, clock part, crystal, findings.

LEFT: *Steampunk Ring.* Amber, antique watch movement, copper, findings.
ABOVE: *Steampunk Bracelet.* Antique watch movement, reptile taxidermy glass eye, vintage button, crystal, copper, clock parts, findings.

ABOVE: *Steampunk Necklace.* Amber, antique
watch movement, brass, copper, findings.
RIGHT: *Steampunk Bracelet.* Antique pocket watch
movement, brass, copper, findings.

ABOVE: *Steampunk Spider Watch Pin.* Watch,
taxidermy glass eye, clock parts, copper, findings.
RIGHT: *Steampunk Ring.* Lab-created opals, copper,
findings.

DR BRASSY STEAMINGTON

"I am one of the oldest makers in steampunk," says California-based Dr Brassy, "I have been making since the late 1980s, long before the movement was called 'Steampunk'. It wasn't until 2008, when I met Nick and Scott, of The League of S.T.E..A.M fame, at the Labyrinth of Jareth Ball in L.A. that I understood there were others like me out there." She works from 'The Lab', her dedicated studio space on the central Californian coast. The work hours are punishing – 7am to 10pm, six days a week. Her main tools are a drill press ('Prissy') and a 2-ton arbor press ('Tony'). Everything in The Lab is steampunk, from the octagonal window to the floor: "there is almost as much metal on the floor as on my work bench." Her materials are all US-made. Brassy has an international client base peppered with celebrities that she is too discreet to mention. Her work is also prized by steampunk insiders, including Steamgirl Kato, Lady Clankington, Thomas Willeford and models Ulorin Vex and La Esmeralda. Her work has appeared extensively, including in magazines *Dark Beauty*, *Gothic Beauty* and *Ladies of Steampunk*, as well as on BBC TV.

LEFT: *Sightmares Bronzeous Mindseye Pin.*
Brass, enamel and glass.

ABOVE: *Portal and Propeller Pins.* Brass, glass,
antique watch gears.
RIGHT: *Gilded Gearess Choker.* Brass and glass.

LEFT: *Leo in the garden*, necklace. Brass, Czech glass, cathedral beads.
ABOVE: Ulorin Vex wearing *Sightmares Pocket Watchers Eye*. Brass, leather, glass.

LEFT: *Sightmares Pocket Watcher Eyes.*
Brass, leather, glass.

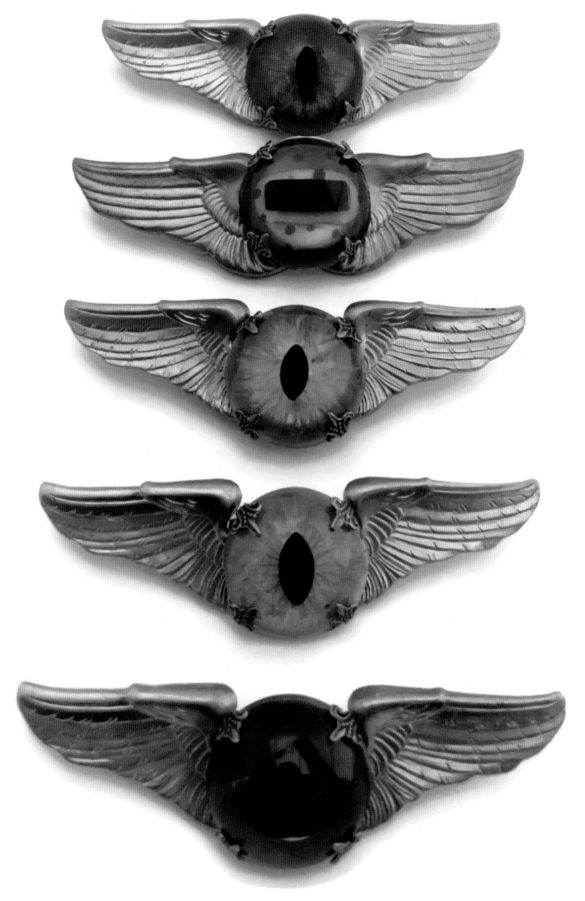

Growing up in Europe as well as the US gave Elaina " a sumptuous taste for the Old World, with its rich patinas and enduring style." She majored in museum studies and then landed a job as registrar for a historical museum. So all day she was handling vintage objects; it was inevitable that doing this and following her interest in science fiction, "sooner or later would land me in the steampunk world." She has two studios at home near San Francisco – one in the house where she does her creation – and one outside"overlooking an English-style cottage garden, full of collected art supplies and inspiration." Creating jewelry is a natural escape – "each piece spawns a new story in my mind, of other times, places and worlds." Her materials are Czech glass beads, pearls, blown glass and metal pieces. "I love combining unusual components in unexpected ways, to create a feeling or mood. I have a special love for the warmth of antique copper; it comes in so many different shades and tones." Elaina creates pieces to complement any steampunk look, but also wants them "to be worn on most days, injecting quotidien life with a little bit of steampunk."

LEFT: *Dream Traveler's Compass Pendant*. Glass cabochon, antique brass-coloured copper wire, compass image, antique brass chain.
ABOVE: *Stratospheric Escape Hot Air Balloon Earrings*. Blown glass beads, filigree copper baskets, copper wire, French-style ear wires, copper findings, copper bead caps.

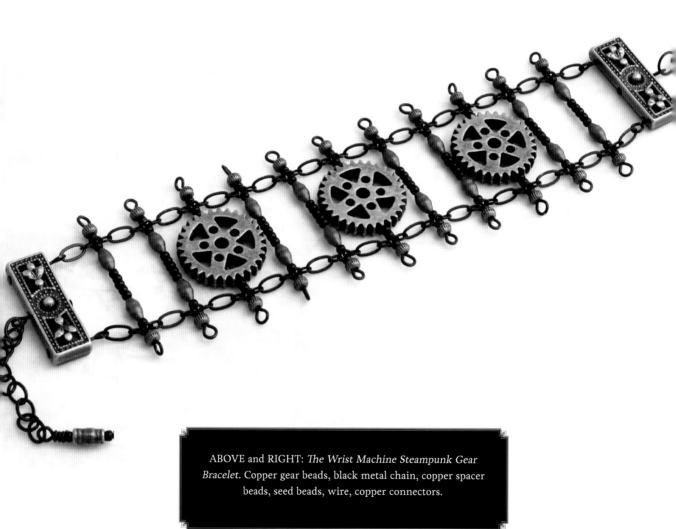

ABOVE and RIGHT: *The Wrist Machine Steampunk Gear Bracelet.* Copper gear beads, black metal chain, copper spacer beads, seed beads, wire, copper connectors.

LEFT: *Cobalt Gamma-Ray Hot Air Balloon Necklace.*
Faceted cobalt blue glass crystal bead, antique brass
findings, fine brass rolo chain.
ABOVE: *Galaxy Traveler Gyro Stabilizer Earrings.* Free-
spinning Picasso Czech glass faceted beads, copper circle
Saturn rings, antique copper lever back ear wires.

"Being born and raised in Hawaii, I learnt the history of the Hawaiian Monarchy of the 19th Century. Royal Hawaiian had close contacts with England's monarchy and made great efforts to bring modern industry, craftsmanship, art and fashion to the islands. Victorian era fashion and art was all the rave at that time." It is the craftsmanship of the period that Friston particularly admires, and which he incorporates in his own work: "there is real beauty in a watch movement, with all its intricate gears and springs." A floral designer for 20 years, Friston now works full time on his jewelry, out of a two-car garage workshop – "a place of escape" – using vintage brass wire, adhesive and Swarovski crystals. He likes designs which represent flight and the workings of clocks, combining these with found pieces of brass with intricate scrollwork. Most of Friston's clients come from overseas; they find him via Etsy and Rebelsmarket.com. He sells to 38 countries, which is enough to "keep me working 12-14 hours per day." Many commissions are for steampunk-themed weddings, and a recent one was a brooch to be worn at the Burning Man festival. The scene on Hawaii is still relatively young – "I only get a few sales from locals" – although that may change with the opening of Gallery Meld in Kailua-Kona, which is featuring many of Friston's jewelry designs.

LEFT: *Pin 054.* Brass, Swarovski crystals.
ABOVE: *Necklace 201.* Silver plate pocket-watch casing, bronze clockface, resin, brass gears, copper-plated key, Swarovski crystals, digital art.

ABOVE: *Cuff 004.* Brass, silver plated brass, copper plated clockface with resin, bronze cast wings, Swarovski crystals.
RIGHT: *Medal 202.* Aluminium hammered wire, silver plated brass, bronze clockface with resin, brass gears, Swarovski crystals.

ABOVE: *Kraken Goggles.* Standard welder's goggles, design paints, acrylic sealer, laser-cut plastic, brass wire, brass and bronze gears, Swarovski crystals.

RIGHT: *Hat Adornment 044.* Bronze cast wings, brass figurals and gears, wooden disc, glass cabochon, aluminum flat wire, tie tacks, Swarovski crystals.

ABOVE: *Heart Pendant.* Bronze filigree, brass gears, Swarovski crystals.
RIGHT: *Pin 309.* Brass, hand-painted glass eye, bronze wings, brass chain, Swarovski crystals.

Fran Horne works, in Worcester, UK, out of a studio at the back of the shop, Curiouser and Curiouser, that she co-owns with artist-maker, Toft Laski. "We both make steampunk, gothic and generally strange items of jewelry, artworks, prints and curios. People who walk in here say it's like a Victorian museum." She has always enjoyed making items from reclaimed and recycled materials, turning unloved items into new exciting and fanciful objects. Fran was always fascinated by vintage scientific and medical ephemera, the result, she thinks, of her previous career as a paramedic. "The effects you get when you cross over science fiction and Victorian and Edwardian aesthetics are also hugely inspiring." The realization that she was working in a steampunk idiom came when she stumbled on the Brass Goggles forum a few years ago and began to meet with other steampunkers. "I then began attending steam rallies and camps, which were still small scale and housed under those old canvas tents." She works with cast resin, creating moulds with unusual or unexpected objects. Sometimes great pieces emerge where the resin casting hasn't worked as intended. Commissions come from individual steampunkers, including work for steampunk-themed weddings. Of the scene, Fran says "It's important that the designer-maker remains at the heart of the movement."

LEFT: *Hand of the Argonauts.* Resin, reclaimed watch parts, vintage finds.
ABOVE: *Aviator Pin.* Brass.

LEFT: *Time in Hand.* Resin, brass, found watch
parts.
ABOVE: *Twilight Time.* Resin, watch parts, brass.

"Being able to breathe life back into something old and discarded is what really inspired me about steampunk.... it also suits my tinkering and romantic nature rather well," says Sneek, Netherlands-based Marija Jillings of Jazz Steampunk. She first got into the scene in 2009, when she and her husband were just starting to make jewelry. After stumbling on an article on steampunk in a magazine, they made a trial line in the genre, and never looked back. Marija works mostly with vintage watch and clock parts and then steel, aluminum and fine epoxy resin. "Using several metals allows a broader choice of colours, and I also like to give our clients that choice." A prodigious worker – "sometimes when I am on a roll, I will work 15-hour days without really noticing" – Marija works with hammer, jeweler's saw and a dremel, as well as "an endless supply of micro screwdrivers for opening up watches and clocks." Much of her work is to commission. The scene in the Netherlands is steadily growing, she says, with events such as the Dutch European Steampunk Convention, held in Meppel. Jazz Steampunk showcase their work all over Europe, at art exhibitions, artisan fairs and fashion shows as well as steampunk conventions. They also participated in L' Artigiano in Fiera in Milan recently, where, over a period of nine days, over 3 million people visited.

LEFT: *Clockwork Spring*. Vintage watch parts, brass, stainless steel, fine epoxy resin.
ABOVE: *Ra's Chariot*. Vintage watch parts, brass, fine epoxy resin.

LEFT: *Sweet Endeavours*. Vintage watch parts, brass, fine epoxy resin.

o ABOVE: *The Inner Workings*. Vintage watch parts, brass, fine epoxy resin.

LEFT: *Around the World in 80 Days.* Vintage watch parts, brass, fine epoxy resin.
ABOVE: *Wild, Wild West.* Vintage watch parts, brass, fine epoxy resin.

ABOVE: *Aphrodite's Sigil.* Vintage watch parts, brass, fine
epoxy resin.
RIGHT: *Gaia's Wealth.* Vintage watch parts, brass, glass.

"Steampunk is eclectic. I enjoy the science fiction and fantasy aspects of it as I can take my creations in many directions, whilst maintaining cohesion," says California-based Susan Ciano Rodgers of Lucky Steampunk. Like many designers she was designing in the idiom and only realized it was in a steampunk vein when she stumbled on others doing the same. She works from her home studio, with her electric dremel, tweezers, round-nose and needle-nose pliers and side cutters. "I am very spiritual, so my workbench is right next to an altar I created. The altar includes all those things that make me feel closer to my higher power – the universe and God. That's where I get my inspiration. If I get creative block, I stop and meditate for a while." The many materials she works with include vintage watch movements, gears, crystals, skulls, charms, nuts, bolts, and screws – "I like the mechanical feel of them." One speciality is her metal cuffs – "they're a hit with my buyers" – and a recent commission was for some steampunk wrist cuffs with hanging chains and spikes for a live action role-play: "....she was depicting a steampunk goddess trying to get beamed back to her spaceship." Interestingly Susan doesn't really plug into her local scene. "There are a few local groups, such as the Fresno Gaslamp Society; I just haven't gotten round to joining!"

LEFT: *Chaos Timepiece Necklace.*
Mixed metal gears, vintage timepiece, mixed charms.
ABOVE: *Timepiece Elegance Bracelet and Ring Set.*
Rhinestones, vintage timepiece, Swarovski crystals.

LEFT: *Time Keeper Metal Cuff.* Metal cuff, gears,
vintage timepiece, clock key.
ABOVE: *Mechanical Skull Flower Necklace.* Filigree
flowers, watch movement pieces, crossbone skull.

ABOVE: *Mechanical Jewels Ring, Cuff and Bracelet.*
Vintage watch parts, gears.
RIGHT: *Flying Wings With Watch Movement
Necklace.* Vintage silver wings, watch movement,
Swarovski rhinestones, brass wings, chain, crystals.

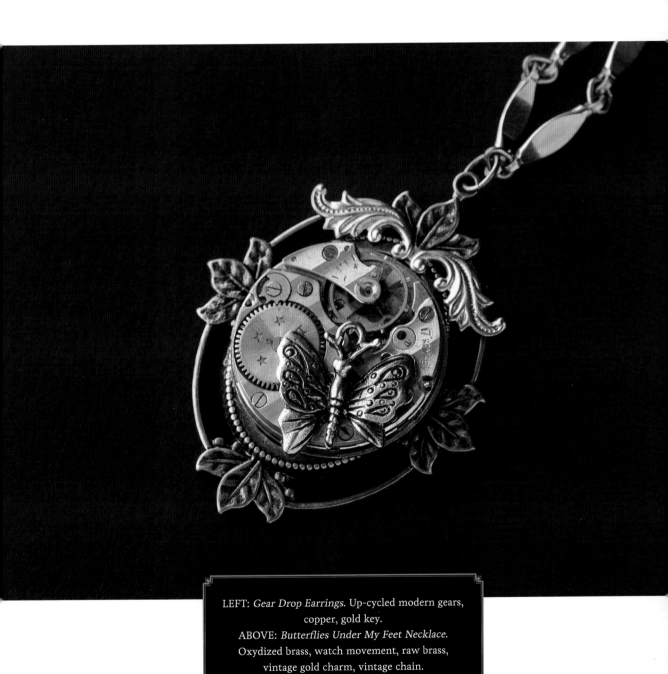

LEFT: *Gear Drop Earrings.* Up-cycled modern gears, copper, gold key.
ABOVE: *Butterflies Under My Feet Necklace.* Oxydized brass, watch movement, raw brass, vintage gold charm, vintage chain.

ABOVE: *Batwing Necklace.* Silver-oxydized brass,
Swiss jeweled watch movement, silver-toned chain.
RIGHT: *Rat Skull and Gears Necklace.* Vintage brass,
rat skull (cruelty-free), watch gears, Czech glass
beads, resin, brass chain.

Based in Montgomeryville, PA, Mechanique Steampunk was established in 2010 by partners Megg and Sean Sweeney; Megg focuses on the jewelry designs whilst Sean concentrates on creating lamps. When it comes to jewelry, Megg wants to achieve "a highly modern aesthetic, with old world taste." The pieces are influenced by steampunk and Victorian gothic, but also have "a hint of heavy metal and rock 'n' roll mixed in." Megg favors detailed watch movements that they pick out for themselves. "We like NOS (new old stock) movements – ones that were made at the factory but never used. We clean them ourselves, whilst ensuring that we retain any patina – that's what gives each individual jewelry piece its unique character." Their established fan base includes steampunk insiders such as Christina Scabbia of Lacuna Coil and Melora Creagar of Rasputina.

ABOVE: *Filigree Necklace.* Vintage brass, Swiss jeweled watch movement, brass chain.

BELOW: *Seampunk Plugs.* Surgical steel, jewelry resin, found watch parts.

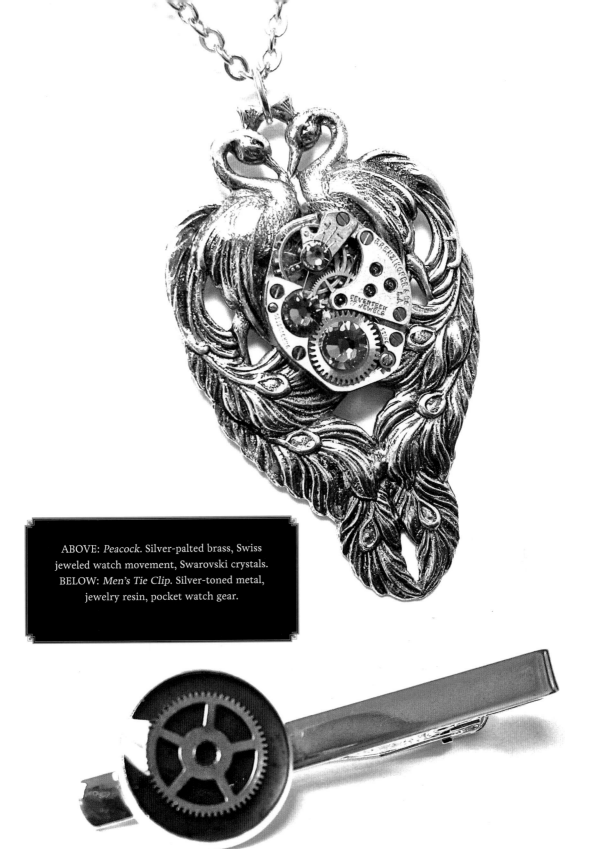

ABOVE: *Peacock*. Silver-palted brass, Swiss
jeweled watch movement, Swarovski crystals.
BELOW: *Men's Tie Clip*. Silver-toned metal,
jewelry resin, pocket watch gear.

ABOVE: *Time Flies Necklace.*
Copper, Swiss jeweled pocket watch
movement, gunmetal chain.
BELOW: *Gear Bracelet.* Silver-toned
metal, jewelry resin, watch gears.

ABOVE: *Victorian-Inspired Necklace.*
Vintage brass, jeweled watch movement,
Swarovski crystals, brass chain.
BELOW: *Steampunk Cufflinks.* Swiss
squared watch movements, silver-toned
cufflink bases, Swarovski crystals.

"I started creating for pleasure and then got carried away," says Tel Aviv-based Orion of Orion's Factory. The attraction to steampunk is well thought through. "Time is lucid and enchanting; creating art with the concept of time in mind is fascinating. There is something about the Victorian, the gothic and the use of cogs in modern day dress which is oddly beautiful." Orion uses Swarovski crystals, casting resin, black chains and cogwheels in her work. Her inspiration

initially was her artistic mother; more recently it's a gothic version of *Alice in Wonderland*. The steampunk scene and goth scenes in Israel are very connected. "There are many steampunkers in my hometown of Tel Aviv and I have found a lot of outlets

for my work. I sell through Etsy and Facebook, but have also had my work shown on many blogs, in newspapers and digital magazines." Orion thinks steampunk has a great future. "The love of Victorian retro isn't going away. There's a continuing interest in a certain nobility of dressing. Even in the mainstream, people are enjoying the unique steampunk look. I know that there are lots of potential new adherents out there also."

LEFT and ABOVE: *Mechanica*, shoulder piece. Black colored chains, computer core, brass cog wheel, Swarovski crystal.

ABOVE: *The Factory*, necklace. Light plastic cog
wheels, abalone gemstone.
RIGHT: *Nobility*, necklace. Brass decorative cog
wheels, Swarovski crystals.

LEFT: *The Seducer*, bracelet. Black lace, brass cog wheels, black colored chains, brass ring.
ABOVE: *The Temptress Tail*, spine/rib piece. Black colored chains, brass cog wheels, brass filigree.

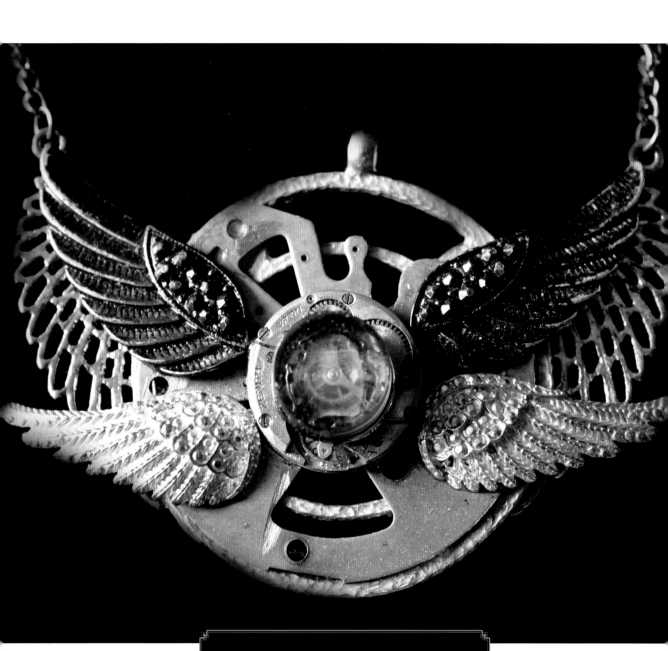

ABOVE: *The Guardian*, pendant. Mechanical clock
plate, watch movement, brass, glass.
RIGHT: *St Mort*, rosary. Blue Czech crystal, Cameo
brass setting, mechanical watch parts, color-shifting
Swarovski crystals.

ABOVE: *Sistema*, kinetic ring. Platinum, semi-precious stone, crystals.

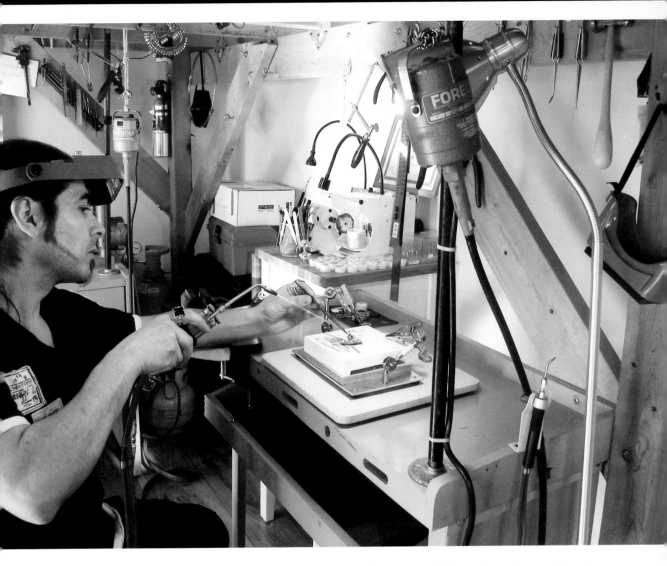

As a boy, Claudio was fascinated by the world of Jules Verne. However, it was the work of Japanese film director, Hayao Miyazaki, which brought him into the steampunk movement. "Animated movies like *Nausica of the Valley of the Wind* and *Laputa - Castle in the Sky* are what rooted me in the scene." Claudio has been creating jewelry profesionally since 1995. "I like to emphasize contrasts between dark and light, hard and soft, tough and tender. When you add steampunk to the mix, you get that unique fusion of yesterday and tomorrow." Claudio's workshop is a 12-foot high loft on the fourth floor of an industrial building in downtown Montreal. Inside he has built a large six foot high structure for displaying his collection of meteorites. "My workshop tools are attached to its ceiling; being inside is like being inside a boat sailing across the sky." Claudio works mainly with precious metals – platinum, gold and silver. He is interested in juxtapositions, "for instance, cold silver on warm brass and copper." Hinged rings recall medieval suits of armor.

Other works explore sensations of precision, expression and precious embellishment. Hugely fêted, Claudio's work has been chosen to represent Canada at the Cheongju International Craft Biennale (Korea, 2009), at the 2010 Vancouver Olympic Winter Games Exhibition and was featured in the *Out of this Space* show in NYC (2013). Several of his rings were also worn by Stanley Tucci's characters in the *Hunger Games* sequel.

LEFT: *Infinity*, kinetic ring. Gold,
silver, blue opal, brass.
ABOVE: *Metamorphosis*, kinetic
ring. Gold, silver, blue opal, pearls,
crystals.

ABOVE and RIGHT: *Tactus*, hinged ring. Gold,
silver, blue opals, crystal.

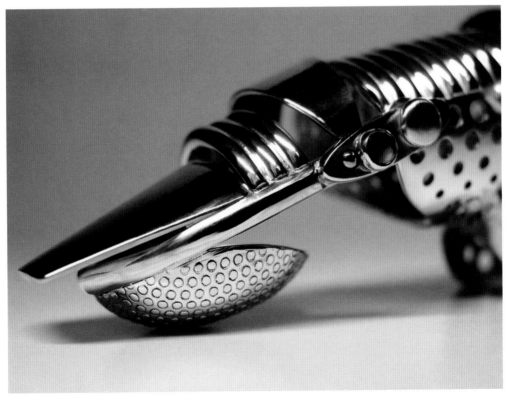

ABOVE: *Philomène*, ring. Platinum and
crystal.
RIGHT: *Interactive Mirror*, kinetic ring.
Gold, silver, pearl, glass, crystal.

Old French fashion magazines from the 1890s to the 1920s are Raven Eve's, (a.k.a Emily Sullivan) main source of inspiration. She doesn't recall how she got into the scene, only saying "it was a mixture of accident and appropriation.... my work just sort of fitted into the whole steampunk thing." She works from a studio in Detroit, Michigan, "crammed to the gills with all sorts of vintage and antique beads, metal stampings and tools I have collected over the years." Like any professional jeweler, Raven Eve isn't just concerned with the aesthetics of her pieces. "Balance and function are top of my list when I design. A piece can look great as you're building it, but if you don't tailor it properly to the part of the body where it will be worn, it will be unwearable." She uses many techniques: metalsmithing, sewing, embroidery, bead work and lampworking glass; "my favourite bits of kit are my soldering equipment and glass torches." Her materials are mostly vintage or antique – better quality she thinks, and also better for the environment. Raven Eve's work has been shown extensively, has been used in movies and by many bands in music videos. She also counts a number of celebrities amongst her clients, as well as steampunk fashion designers including Lipservice Clothing. Her advice? "Dress up, even if just a little, every day!"

LEFT: *Dark Fairy Ear Cuff*. Vintage sequins, antique silver filigree.
ABOVE: *Circus Kei Headdress*. Antique and new lace, vintage plastic, antique glass pearls.

LEFT: *Tribal Brass Gypsy Bib Necklace.*
Vintage brass, vintage glass stones, lead
crystal beads.
ABOVE: *Ambergris Art Nouveau
Headdress.* Vintage brass, gold tone
chain, glass beads.

Based in Lexington NC, April Everhart of the Steampunk Movement, describes herself as "just a southern country girl with an obsession for steampunk." She came across the movement online and then started experimenting with some antique watch movements from her local market. "Taking them apart with the miniature tools I bought was like opening a Christmas present – you never know what you'll find inside." She works through a process she calls 'cluttered creativity', where she lays all her supplies on her work bench and then creates ten pieces at a time. "I use dials, movements, tiny gears mixed with different metals like brass copper and silver and then add colour and a touch of bling with crystals."

Of Lexington she says "there is no steampunk scene at all! Only southern country life in NC! Most locals have no idea what steampunk is." She sells on Etsy and "at a local artists' emporium". Many of her clients are young locals, who just like her jewelry. She has also sold to musicians – one of her pocket watch necklaces was featured in a video for the band Chelsea Grin.

LEFT: *Holding Time*, necklace. Filigree setting, metal watch face, brass finding, glass crystal.
ABOVE: *Bee Fly*, necklace. Brass, vintage pocket watch movement, brass finding, brass chain.

LEFT: *Etched Elgin*, necklace. Vintage pocket
watch movement, filigree setting, chain.
ABOVE: *Blooming Beauty*, necklace. Vintage pocket
watch movement, brass findings, colored crystals.

ABOVE: *Ringer*, ring. Metal ring setting, oval vintage watch movement, brass finding.
RIGHT: *Aged Elegance*, necklace. Vintage pocket watch, brass, watch movements, watch dials, chain, brass findings.

Maria Sparks is a watchmaker by training, as well as a jeweler. "I found the steamunk genre on the web about seven years ago and just fell in love with it. It's the perfect outlet for combining the interests of a watchmaker and jewelry artist." Based in Oregon, she loves Victoriana, art nouveau, art deco and science fiction; "my trade also means I am fascinated with anything that functions with gears." Maria creates on an antique workbench, with antique watch repair tools, in a studio with massive windows and views of the mountains. She uses watches that are no longer repairable – "it has to be that they can no longer function as viable timepieces. As you can see I am rather fond of watches." Her main inspirations, she says, are the art and design of the Victorian and art nouveau periods. "However, when I sit down to create, I find that the watch mechanism – the shape of the gear plates, the arrangement of the exposed gearing and the age of the watch, become my direct source of ideas." A recent favorite piece incorporated antique brass clock gears, two handmade Swiss pocket watches from the 1880s, vintage jewelry pieces, black crystal beads and glass vials filled with watch parts. Maria lives near Portland where "luckily there are lots of true steampunk enthusiasts." She sells his work mostly online on Etsy, but also in local galleries and boutiques.

LEFT: *Untitled*, necklace. 1900s Elgin pocket watch movement, copper, Swarovksi faceted crystal beads, Swarovski crystal stones.
ABOVE: *Untitled*, necklace. 1890s pocket watch, freshwater coin pearl, antiqued brass, skeleton key charm.

ABOVE: *Untitled*, pendant. 1890s antique pocket watch, faceted blue sapphire, vintage steel pocket watch gears, blue sapphire winding crown, brass filigree.

RIGHT: *Untitled*, necklace. 1930s 14k gold engraved wristwatch case, 1920s ladies Elgin pocket watch, vintage steel watch gears, faceted garnet, faceted ruby, antique silver figural, Swarovski crystals, faceted red crystal drops, antique brass filigree.

ABOVE: *Untitled.* 1930s art deco 14k white gold pocket watch case, 1900s pocket watch (fully restored; can be worn with mechanism running), vintage steel watch gears, Swarovski crystal stones, antiqued silver filigree, freshwater pearls.

RIGHT: *Untitled,* necklace. 1910s Waltham pocket watch, amethyst gemstone beads, silver filigree, freshwater pearls, vintage steel watch gears, Swarovski crystals, amethyst briolette drop, two Swiss 1940s watch movements.

ABOVE: *Untitled.* 1920s nickel watch case, created red ruby stone, antiqued brass, brass and steel watch gears, black crystal beads.
RIGHT: *Untitled.* 1910s Waltham watch movement, antique crystal beads, antiqued silver filigree, vintage steel watch gear set, zirconia stone, Swarovsky crystal beads.

ABOVE: *Nautilus Flare*, pin. Laser-cut
stained wood, patina paint, brass screws.
RIGHT: *Rose Pendant.*
Laser-cut stained wood.

In 2012 Greg and Lora Price attended, by chance, the Clockwork Alchemy convention in San Jose, CA. What they saw inspired them so much that, at the end of their day there, Steamy Tech was born. Their workshop is in a maker space called TechShop in San Jose, where they can make use of kit like the 60W Epilog lasers to cut all their wooden items. "Those lasers are amazing – they allow a level of precision that wouldn't be remotely possible using hand tools." Always keen to embrace new technology, Steamy Tech have also been using the MarketBot Replicator, a 3-D printer, for acrylic items. Most of their work is in wood, but "we like acrylic for light pieces – we can always paint it to look metallic." The creative vibe of TechShop is a spur to creativity, as is the very supportive Bay Area steampunk community. "There is the Steam Federation – Bay Area, that meets weekly; there are many steampunk groups all the way from Santa Cruz to Sacramento; and then there are the conventions (we love taking our 3-D printer to those) like Steamstock, Convolution, Nova Albion and, of course, Clockwork Alchemy." Steamy Tech sell on Etsy, but love seeing their work in stores like Otherworlds in Edmonds, WA or Discover San Jose. They see technology as helping the "community of makers create the world of manners, style and imagination we want to live in."

ABOVE: *Heart*, pin. Laser-cut
stained wood, brass screws.

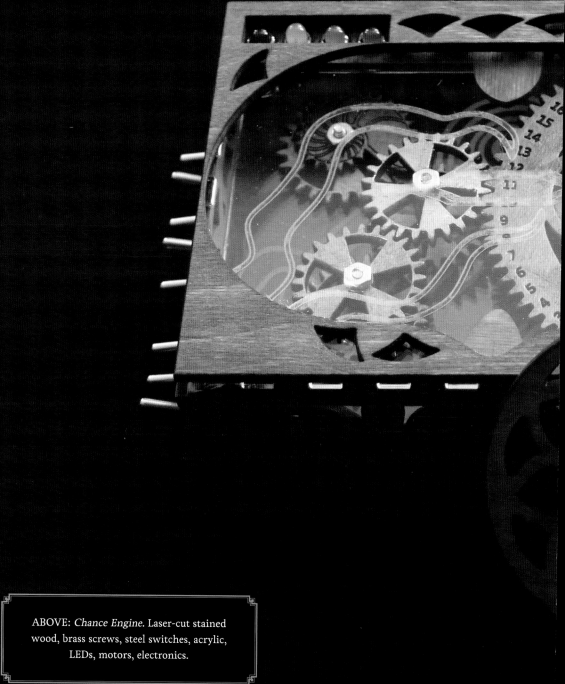

ABOVE: *Chance Engine.* Laser-cut stained
wood, brass screws, steel switches, acrylic,
LEDs, motors, electronics.

ABOVE: *Untitled*, earrings. Acrylic, patina paint,
feathers, metal clips.
RIGHT, TOP: *Steamstock Pendant.* Laser-cut stained
wood, metal chain.
RIGHT: *Ornaments.* Laser-cut stained wood.

ABOVE AND RIGHT: *Mechanical Heart.* Brass, copper, electrical supplies, watch gears, copper chain.

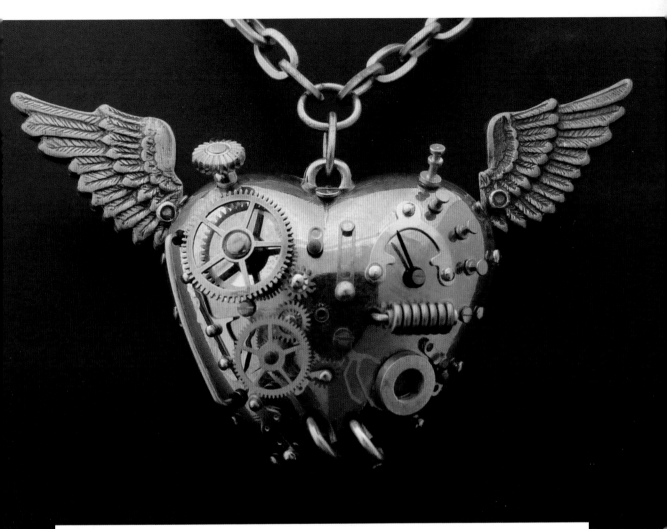

"I just love the fantasy and mystery of steampunk" says Michelle Murray of Perth, Australia's Steel Hip. "I make a complex little machine and then leave it to the wearer to imagine what it does and how it does it. Luckily with steampunk we don't have to follow the laws of physics, biology or thermodynamics." She remembers as a child seeing a singing bird automaton. "It wasn't the bird that overawed me, but the mechanism and craftsmanship." Like many steampunkers she was creating in the idiom when by chance, looking for supplies online, she stumbled on the term and the community. She sees steampunk as an antidote to the mass-produced junk sold in malls the world over. "Steampunk could be our Arts and Crafts Movement; why does our technology have to be so disposable and bland ?" Her studio is scattered with her many supplies, part of what she describes as her "autocreative chaos." When, aged 20 and following a hip replacement, Michelle suffered a fall and broke her right wrist. "It had to be surgically fused with a steel plate and seven long screws. This keeps my hand really level when I work with my drills and I don't suffer fatigue." With materials she searches out new old US stock from the '40s and '50s, or imported parts from Europe. Inspiration is from "everywhere", but she names the work of Fornasetti and Kris Kuski in particular. Steel Hip sells worldwide, and recently had pieces exhibited in the Antipodean Steampunk Show.

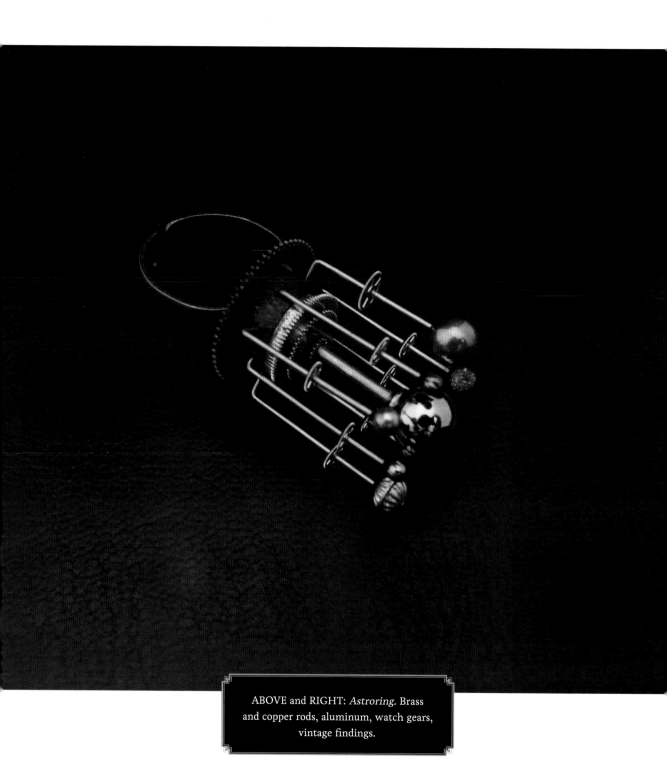

ABOVE and RIGHT: *Astroring.* Brass
and copper rods, aluminum, watch gears,
vintage findings.

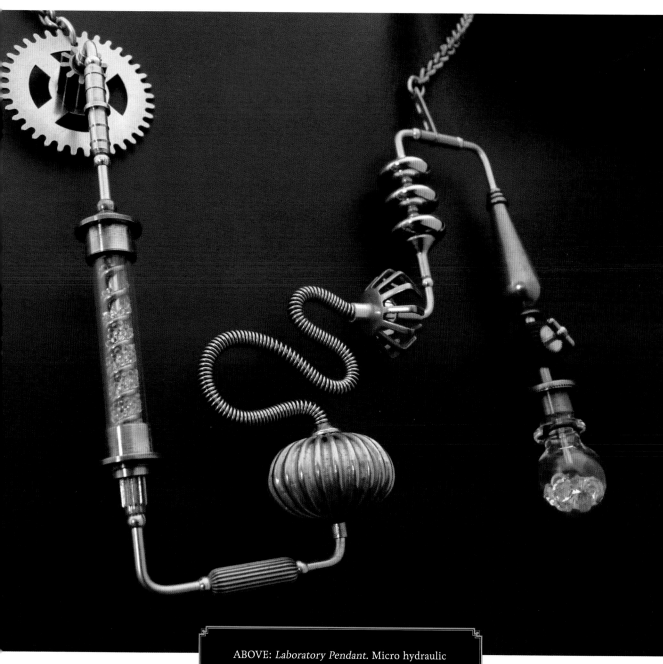

ABOVE: *Laboratory Pendant.* Micro hydraulic
fittings, copper tubing, brass gears.
RIGHT: *Reactor Pendant.* Micro hydraulic fittings,
brass tubing, brass gears.

LEFT and ABOVE: *Heart in Dock.* Brass, brass and steel gears, copper chain.

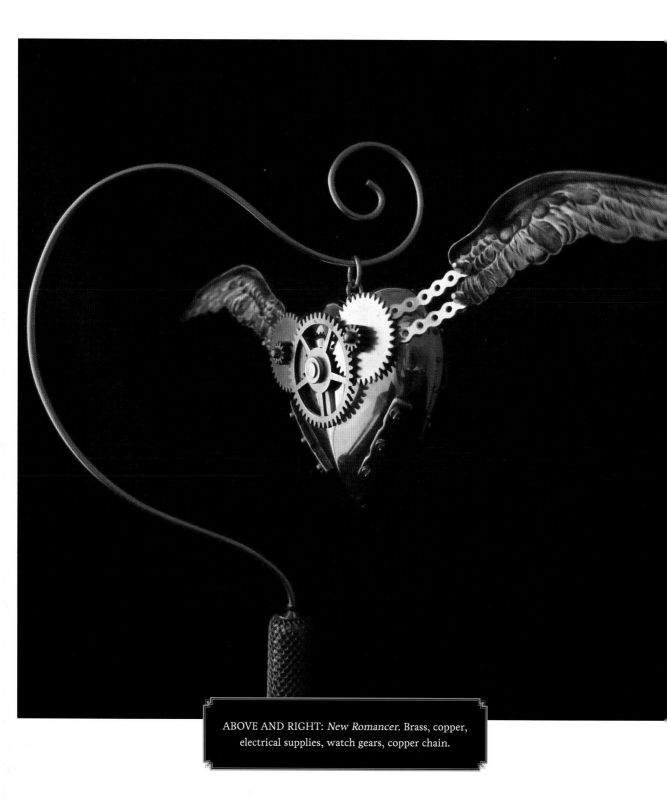

ABOVE AND RIGHT: *New Romancer*. Brass, copper, electrical supplies, watch gears, copper chain.

ABOVE: *Art Deco Steampunk Gear Scene Ring.*
Sterling silver.
RIGHT: *Steampunk Nuts and Bolts Gear Ring.*
Sterling silver.

A family-owned business, Gary Swank Jewelers have been based on Broadway in Portland, Oregon since 1973. The business, started by Gary Swank, has grown steadily and in the last three years Gary's son and daughter joined and introduced a steampunk aesthetic – and the marque of Swank Metalsmithing – into the product line. "It was on Etsy that I first stumbled on some images of steampunk jewelry," says Chelsea, "and I immediately fell in love." It is the obscurity of steampunk that she loves, and the fact that "it isn't mainstream, but retains an underground quality which keeps it ellusive and sexy. I love too the way it's undefined, and yet you know something is steampunk if you see it." Today the shop has a definite steampunk quality. "We have a large, recycled piece of perforated steel that we use to hang all our tools from and work tables which resemble gears, made by a local welder. The shop is totally open, so that people can watch us work, cast and see all the tools that we use." They work mostly in sterling silver, yellow, green, white and rose gold, palladium and platinum. "We work with these metals because we know them deeply, and know how to cast them, which is imperative for our highly-detailed designs." Inspiration comes from many sources: from old watch parts to train tracks, Art Deco to Art Nouveau and also, in Chelsea's case, from Egyptian Revival designs. They have many fans in Portland, where the steampunk scene is strong: "the other day on the MAX train I was captivated by a girl with the most amazing black leather steampunk boots. They had a platform heel, large buckles going all the way up her leg, with little gears riveted into the sole. So cool, but not an untypical occurrence in Portland."

ABOVE: *Steampunk Gears and Rivets Ring.* 14k gold.

LEFT: *Gears, Grooves and Grates Steampunk Ring.*
Sterling silver.
ABOVE: *Victorian Silver Cocktail Ring.*
Sterling silver.

ABOVE: *Gears, Grates and Rivets Steampunk Pendant.* Sterling silver.

LEFT: *Derek Foster's Custom Gear Ring.* 14k rose
gold, palladium, 14k white gold.
ABOVE: *Stacking Steampunk Gears and Rivets Ring.*
Sterling silver, rose cut black diamond.

LEFT: *Antique Watch Dial Pendant and Earring Set.* Sterling silver, freshwater pearls, onyx, antique watch gears.
ABOVE: *Gears, Grooves and Grates Steampunk Ring.* Sterling silver.

APPENDIX

PHOTOGRAPHY, STYLING, APPAREL AND MODEL CREDITS.
FOR FURTHER DETAILS PLEASE CONTACT THE ARTISTS.

P. 14

Model: Cristina Peterson
Photography & Jewelry: Bionic Unicorn
Circlet: Organic Armor
Blouse: Blasphemina's Closet
Hair & Makeup: Penny Dreadful

p.16

Model/Hair/Makeup: Penny Dreadful
Photography: Amy Ballinger
Ram Horn Circlet: Organic Armor
Corset: Scoundrelle's Keep
Skirt: KMK Designs

p. 17

Model: Cristina Peterson
Photography: Amy Ballinger
Unicorn Circlet: Organic Armor
Blouse: Black Milk
Hair: Zoe Copoulus
Makeup: Leanne Skar

p. 19

Model/Hair/Makeup: Penny Dreadful
Photography & Jewelry: Bionic Unicorn
Hat & Corset: Organic Armor
Blouse: Blasphemina's Closet
Skirt: KMK Designs

p. 21

Model: Penny Dreadful
Clothing: Custom designed leather leaf crown and
feather adorned Steampunk harness by The Artificer's
Aethernautical Emporium.
Hair and Make-up: Amber Rose Hair + Makeup

p. 43

Model: Dr Brassy Steamington
Photography: Mindseye Photography

p.47

Model: Ulorin Vex
Photography: Julian M Kilsby

p. 94, 95, 98, 99

Model: Yune Nirzhberg
Photography: Julie Teitler
Jewelry: Orion's Factory Jewelry
Make Up: Noga Levin Make-up
Styling: Gale Dulev
Hair: Ira Bash & Noga Levin
orionsfactoryjewelry.com